D1606603

Pebble® Plus

Health and Your **Body**

How Your Body Works

by Rebecca Weber

CAPSTONE PRESS
a capstone imprint

Pebble Plus is published by Capstone Press,
151 Good Counsel Drive, P.O. Box 669, Mankato, Minnesota 56002.
www.capstonepub.com

Books published by Capstone Press are manufactured with paper
containing at least 10 percent post-consumer waste.

Library of Congress Cataloging-in-Publication Data
Weber, Rebecca.
  How your body works / by Rebecca Weber
    p. cm. — (Pebble plus. Health and your body)
  Includes bibliographical references and index.
  ISBN 978-1-4296-6609-1 (library binding)
  1. Human physiology—Juvenile literature. 2. Human anatomy—Juvenile
literature. I. Title.
  QP37.W39 2011
  612—dc22   2010034314

Summary: Simple text and color photographs discuss how the major systems of the human body work.

Editorial Credits
Gillia Olson, editor; Veronica Correia, designer; Svetlana Zhurkin, media researcher; Laura Manthe, production specialist

Photo Credits
BananaStock, 4–5, 12–13
Shutterstock: Alexey Fursov, cover; Benjamin Loo, 10–11; Juan Manuel Ordonez, 20; Mandy Godbehear, 16–17; Maxim
    Slugin, 1; Monkey Business Images, 6–7; Pavel Govorov, 8–9; Rob Marmion, 18–19; Tihis, 21; wavebreakmedia, 14–15

Note to Parents and Teachers

The Health and Your Body series supports national standards related to health and physical
education. This book describes and illustrates how the human body works. The images support
early readers in understanding the text. The repetition of words and phrases helps early readers
learn new words. This book also introduces early readers to subject-specific vocabulary words,
which are defined in the Glossary section. Early readers may need assistance to read some
words and to use the Table of Contents, Glossary, Read More, Internet Sites, and Index sections
of the book.

Printed in the United States of America in North Mankato, Minnesota.
092010
005933CGS11

Table of Contents

Your Body

Your body is just like a factory.

A soda can factory takes in

metal and turns it into cans.

Your body takes in food and air.

It turns them into energy.

Your Busy Brain

Your brain is your body's boss.
This organ tells your body what
to do. It tells your heart to beat.
When you read, your brain tells
you what words your eyes see.

Heart Healthy

Your heart pumps blood through your body. Blood carries oxygen and nutrients. Blood also carries carbon dioxide and other waste to be sent out of the body.

Love Your Lungs

People can't live without air.
Breathing in pulls air
into your lungs to get oxygen.
When you breathe out, your
lungs get rid of carbon dioxide.

The Food Track

Your digestive system takes in nutrients from food. Food moves from the stomach to the small intestine to the blood. Waste goes out through the large intestine.

Sensible Senses

Hearing, smelling, touching, seeing, and tasting are senses. Your senses send information to your brain. They tell you what is going on around you.

Big, Strong Bones

People have about 206 bones.

Your bones support your body.

They keep your organs safe.

Muscles move your bones

by pulling on them.

The Skin You're In

Your skin keeps your blood
and organs inside your body.
It keeps out germs and dirt.
When you play hard, your skin
makes sweat to cool you down.

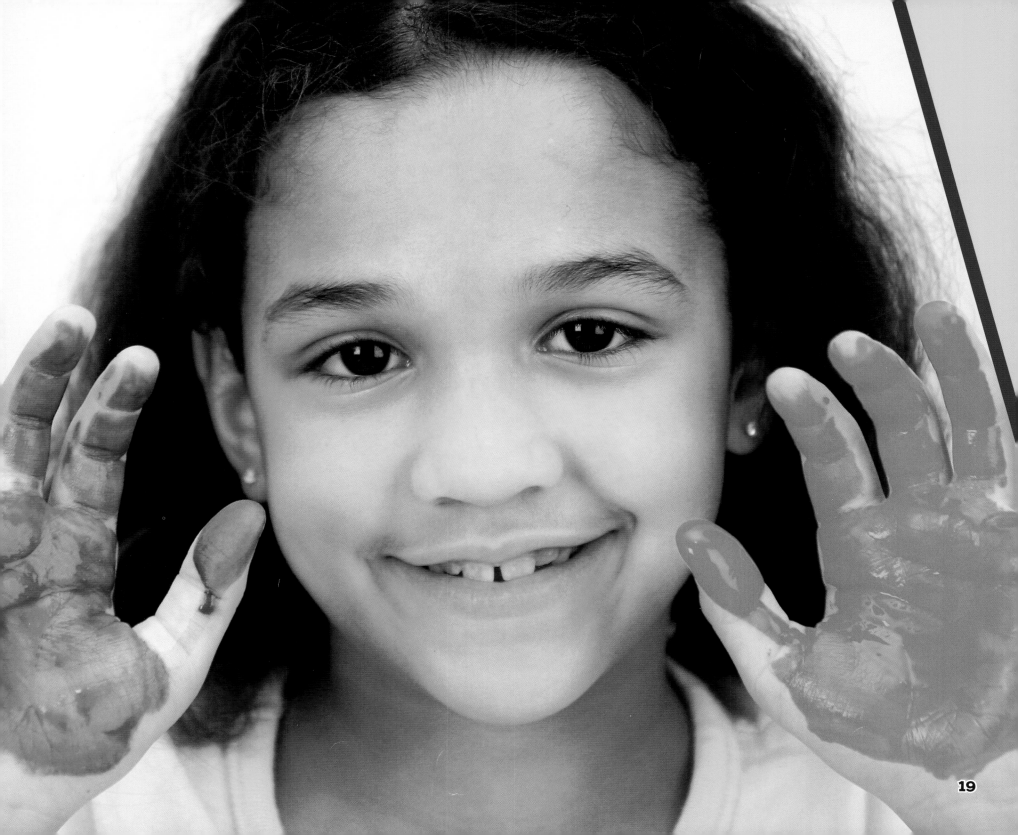

Fun Facts

- The left side of your brain controls the right side of your body. The right side of your brain controls the left side of your body.

- By the time you are 6 years old, your brain weighs about 3 pounds (1.4 kilograms). After that, it doesn't get any heavier.

- Messages to and from your brain can travel more than 200 miles (320 kilometers) per hour.

- Your teeth have different jobs. Front teeth tear food apart. Back teeth mash and grind food so you can swallow it.

- Always try to breathe through your nose. It has thousands of little hairs that trap dust and dirt.

Glossary

carbon dioxide—a colorless, odorless gas that people and animals breathe out as waste

energy—the strength to do active things without becoming tired

germ—very tiny living things that can cause sickness

intestine—a long tube in the body that breaks down food

muscle—a part of the body that makes movement; muscles are attached to bones

nutrient—something that people, plants, and animals need to stay healthy

organ—a part of the body that does a specific job; the heart, lungs, and brain are organs

oxygen—a colorless gas in the air that people and animals need to breathe

Read More

Ardagh, Philip. *Your Body: Boogers and All.* New York : Price Stern Sloan, 2010.

Enslow, Brian. *My Body.* All About My Body. Berkeley Heights, N.J.: Enslow Publishers, 2011.

Smith, Penny, ed. *First Human Body Encyclopedia.* First Reference for Young Readers and Writers. New York: DK Publishing, 2005.

Internet Sites

FactHound offers a safe, fun way to find Internet sites related to this book. All of the sites on FactHound have been researched by our staff.

Here's all you do:

Visit *www.facthound.com*

Type in this code: 9781429666091

Super-cool stuff! Check out projects, games and lots more at **www.capstonekids.com**

23

Index

Word Count: 218 (main text)
Grade: 1
Early-Intervention Level: 22